Kingdom of God

The Parables of
The Sower, The Growing Seed and
The Mustard Seed

Swami Yogeshwarananda

© Swami Yogeshwarananda 2021

The right of Swami Yogeshwarananda to be
identified as the author of this work has been asserted by
him in accordance with the Copyright, Designs and
Patents Act 1988

ISBN: 979- 8763432138
First published in 2021

Divine News Publications

A Note to the Reader

The teachings of Jesus contain a wealth of spiritual wisdom. Unfortunately, however, they have been somewhat overlooked by Christian theologians, scholars and more so the clergy. Consequently, Christian audiences, the world over, are unfamiliar with them.

I have begun to undertake the process of opening out and explaining these teachings through books, seminars and lectures.

• • •

The purpose of this book is to spread the sublime spiritual teachings of Jesus to the world. If you are interested in facilitating this, or resonate with the book's content and want to learn more, you can get in touch by emailing us at:

quest.divinenews@gmail.com

Likewise, if you are interested in viewing the seminars that I have done on the entire Gospel of Matthew as well as the complete Gospel of Mark, which are available at no cost, please get in touch.

Contents

Preface

The four Gospels speak of the science of salvation, as presented by Jesus and not as indicated by the Church with its Church doctrine. The four Gospels should be read, taught and understood as per the teachings of Jesus which are mystically worded and thereby thus far have not been properly opened out to the human race.

The subject and the theme of the four Gospels are meant for the entire human race, irrespective of its religious affiliations. All earnest seekers of God should address the contents of the four Gospels in order to obtain spiritual wisdom, the living of which would lead and propel a person to the ever-sought God-experience.

Jesus' blessed teachings are opened out here, albeit for the first time, as a blessing to the human race, echoing Jesus' words, "*One flock, one shepherd*", which is very true indeed. This will only be possible with the spread of the word, as taught by Jesus in the four Gospels.

The four gospels contain an enlightening, soul-elevating teaching, leading man to the kingdom of God.

The parables of The Sower, The Growing Seed, and The Mustard Seed open out the mystery of redemption, in very innocuous terms, with camouflaged phrases to its mysterious content, so far not deciphered by the Christian world. Its contents would fortify and enhance the minds of Christians, Hindus and Buddhists who quest for salvation.

Introduction

- WHAT and WHERE is the kingdom of God?

- HOW and WHEN will it transpire?

- This process is OUTLINED in the parables of Chapter 4 in the Gospel of Mark.

- WHAT is it?

- God-vision, in contrast to world vision.

- How to maintain the GOD-VISION.

- The true meaning of the HOLY SABBATH which God wanted you to entertain.

- The WAY to manifest the KINGDOM OF GOD is outlined from 4:26-32 in the Gospel of Mark.

- Jesus says: "SO IS THE KINGDOM OF GOD" which he outlines.

- Thus the way to salvation is outlined here.

Part 1
The Seed

In the beginning was the word.

The word was with God.

And the word was God.

And when you hear the word from God, it will make you God.

Chapter 4 of the Gospel of Mark is one of the most significant chapters in the Gospels. For, it opens out the science of getting enlightened. The parable of "The Sower and the Seed", which is given at the start of the chapter, is a very significant parable which outlines and opens out the mystery of the kingdom of God or the mystery of the mystical knowledge that leads a person towards salvation.

Beginning with the parable of The Sower, the science of enlightenment is very beautifully brought out. In the parable, Jesus explains what the seed is, the one who sows it, and the one who receives it, namely the human mortal individual. Thereafter, how the receiver has to permit that seed, which is the word of God, to take root within himself within his own mind structure. Thus that science, or that mystical process, is so ingeniously outlined by Jesus in this parable.

Also, he follows this parable with a very brief statement about the candle and the candlestick as to who and what is the candlestick, and what is the candle. The candle-light is God-awareness. Then he says how, when you lighteth your awareness with God-awareness, what is unmanifest, which is namely the Divine, would get manifest in each individual. And also, at the same time he mentions that your Divine nature, which was kept as a hidden secret from you, gets opened out. The short parable of The Candle and the Candlestick unravels that secret of your Divine Beingness, when you maintain the flame of God-awareness.

And then he follows this up in another little section by stating *how* you maintain, and *where* you should maintain, this God-awareness: He briefly outlines this by mentioning, with what measure you measure things, in the corresponding manner, things will be measured unto you. If you wish to measure the dimensions of your garden, you need a measuring tape. But if you want to measure the universe, you can only measure it with God-awareness. So with this God-awareness, you could measure the universe. And when you do so, with what measure you measure, it will be measured back unto you. Which means that if you were to measure the universe, or, to use another phraseology, to envelope or permeate this entire universe with God-awareness, then with what measure you measure, it will be measured back unto you. So when you measure it with God-awareness, it will be measured back unto you with that God-experience. Similarly also, with respect to yourself, the secret of your beingness would be opened out.

Maintaining God-awareness means the vision of God (the unseen Divine) is maintained in the back of your awareness. A good example for this is a mother who has a new-born baby which lieth in the cot: the mother, despite moving around the house attending to her household chores, always has the baby in the periphery of her awareness, so that, even without seeing the baby, she is aware when it makes even a little hiccup.

So similarly, the unseen God exists, pervading and permeating the entire universe with Its Beingness. When you maintain this God-awareness, i.e. envelop and permeate the entire universe with this God-awareness, then in due course it will get manifest to you as an experience. And this process has to be consistently practiced. And the more you practice, the more capacity will be given unto you. But in case you fail to do so, then what little capacity you have, or what was given to you initially, will fade away. This is very well known to everyone in the practice of whatever craft they have – if they don't keep practicing that craft, then that craft fades away. Similarly, here too also.

Therefore, that's what he says: if you don't maintain this and neglect it, then in due course it fades away from your memory and from your consciousness. But, on the other hand, if you were to maintain it, more will be given to you.

Then he goes on to explain this and further exemplify this truth in the subsequent parables. Because, note that all the parables in Chapter 4 are sequential and linked to the introductory parable of The Sower. As such, Chapter 4 is a very beautiful chapter and one of the most significant chapters which outlines the final essence of your spiritual knowledge.

And Jesus says in line 26:

26*And he said, So is the kingdom of God, as if a man should cast seed into the ground;*

When you put or strew seed into the ground, what happens? In due course, over a period of time, the seed goes through its process in Mother Earth. So also, when this seed of understanding that thou art the Divine is sown in your heart and gets embedded in your mind, it seeds and begins to fructify within you. For, mind is the field in which this seed of God-awareness has been sown. And to exemplify how this happens, Jesus gives you an example of the seed which is put into the ground:

Line 27:

27*And should sleep, and rise night and day, and the seed should spring and grow up, he knoweth not how.*

So when you have put the seed into the ground, and you sleep in the night and rise in the day while going through the process of living life, the seed does not sprout out the next day, but it takes its own time in the bowels of the Earth and goes through a process which is unseen to you.

So also, when this seed of God-awareness (that I am that Divine) is entertained in your mind, it enters the subconscious of your mind, which is likened to the field, and then, in due course, as days and nights come and go, this seed of God-awareness springs and develops automatically over a period of time; just as the seed, which was put into the soil of Mother Earth, over a period of a few days and nights, begins to sprout up and eventually becomes ready to harvest.

But he does not know how. In the same way also, this seed of God-awareness, which has been put into your conscious mind, remains in the subconscious of your mind and begins to spring and grow up. "*He knoweth not how*". But all through, the person is consciously entertaining it and keeping a watch on it.

Then he says in lines 28 and 29:

28For the earth bringeth forth fruit of herself; first the blade, then the ear, after that the full corn in the ear. 29But when the fruit is brought forth, immediately he putteth in the sickle, because the harvest is come.

Similarly also, when you entertain or maintain this God-awareness within yourself in the conscious part of your mind, then in due course, in the subconscious part of the mind, which is likened to the bowels of the Earth, the process is going on whereby the seed of knowledge that "I am that Divine" begins to grow and becomes ready for harvesting. And when the time has come, the harvest takes place. So both in the conscious and subconscious mind, the process is going on.

In Biblical phraseology, the harvest time has been mentioned. Now, what is this harvest time?

It is the time when you are ready for enlightenment… when you are ripe for enlightenment. Now you are on the brink of getting enlightened.

And when does enlightenment take place? It takes place when that "I am that Divine" awareness totally saturates your mind – when your subconscious and unconscious mind gets totally saturated with this impression. At first, it is a conscious impression in the conscious mind, and then as you keep entertaining this impression, gradually it gets into the subconscious of your mind, or the unconscious part of your mind, and fills it up.

The subconscious part of your mind was previously filled with worldly impressions. It was filled with two types of impression. One is the "I am" impression, the ego impression. This impression is demonstrated by asking an ordinary man "who are you?" and he will respond by giving you a big biography about himself where he repeatedly asserts the I ("I am so and so, I am this, I am that",

19

etc.). This is because the I-impression, or the ego-impression, is so strongly embedded in the subconscious of your mind or the unconscious part of your mind. And also, all types of worldly impressions too are embedded there.

Maintaining this God-impression in Hindu technical terminology is called *Brahmakaravritti* – that is a mind-state corresponding to *Brahman*. *Brahman* is the term which has been given in the Hindu structure for the Divine; it is only a term or a word, and not a name, which implies the character and the nature of the Divine, for your human comprehension. Then when that awareness gets entertained by you, it goes to saturate the conscious, subconscious and unconscious parts of your mind. Thus by this process, the worldly impressions which are lying embedded in the subconscious and the unconscious part of your mind along with the ego-impressions which are lying there, get neutralised and cleared: It's like inserting one thorn in to remove another thorn which has got into your foot. So here also, the Godly impressions are going and saturating your mind and subconscious mind, and are clearing away your worldly and ego impressions. And then a time will come when your mind (the subconscious and the conscious part of your mind) is saturated with this "I am the Divine" impression. When that time comes, then you are ready to get enlightened. That is, the time has come for your harvest. ("Harvest" is the Biblical word used in the parables of the four Gospels.)

And, at that time, how does this harvesting take place? For this process, Jesus uses the word "sickle", which is a special curved knife with the help of which one can easily cut the stalk from the stem. So what gets cut on being enlightened?

It is your ego-nature along with your ego-based individuality which gets cut and cleared. The sickle is used to denote this process – the cutting is just an expression used to show the ego is no more. This is how you lose your ego. When you lose your ego, you will find true life. That is why Jesus says that when you lose yourself, you will find true life (Gospel of Matthew, 16:25).

Losing yourself is a subtle process. But in order to lose yourself, you must be prepared to lose yourself. One young man went to a well-known but rough Zen teacher and asked, "can you show me the quickest way to get enlightened?" and prompt came the reply from the teacher, "get lost". The young man was baffled, thinking to himself, "I went with all respect to get a teaching, and he tells me 'get lost'". Later on, it was explained to the young man that to "get lost" means to lose yourself. Thus in enlightenment, practically you are losing yourself; thus at that point the sickle has been put.

Now, we will go one step further in demonstrating how this sickle gets used, which we will do so by illustrating an incident that took place in the 20th Century...

Yoga Swami was a saint who resided in Jaffna, Sri Lanka. (Note, a saint is a person who has had the Divine-experience, i.e. the experience that "I am God", and numerous terms are used to denote this experience, such as God-realisation, Self-realisation, Godly-experience, getting enlightened, obtaining *Nirvana* – these are all synonymous terms.) As a young man, over one hundred years ago, he worked in a government office in the forest area in the irrigation department and was in charge of the stores and was doing his work very meticulously and carefully. He was also living a very exemplary life: he was correct in everything that he did, was correct as a person, and was correct in his dealings and interactions with fellow people. Thus he was also very correct in his job too. So his superior officer, who happened to be an Englishman, observed his behaviour and made the remark to him:

"*You are a perfect man.*" (Note, he didn't say "a perfect god"; he said "a perfect man".) He was a perfect man because he was living a perfect life and was correct in everything that he was doing and no fault could be found in him. He was also, at the same time, going through his spiritual practices. Then in due course, having becoming deeply immersed in his spiritual practices, one fine day he went to meet his future guru, Chellappa Swami: The moment the guru saw the disciple, he said with a great deal of power in his voice in his native Tamil language: "*Yar ada nee?*" That means: "*Who the Dickens are you?*"

Then and there the future disciple realised who he really was, that is who he really is. And Yoga Swami subsequently said, "*at that very moment I realised who I was; who I am*". For, what had happened at that moment, was the sickle was put to the harvest, as he was spiritually ready, and his ego character was cut off. Thus he got disconnected with the ego identification and had the Divine experience that "I am that". Therefore, that is the meaning of the statement of Jesus when he said, *"the sickle is put when the harvest has come"*.

For, the parable of The Growing Seed is being explained and opened out to you with the phrase "the harvest is ready for the sickle to be used". And Jesus in lines 30-32 says:

[30]*And he said, Whereunto shall we liken the kingdom of God? or with what comparison shall we compare it?* [31]It is *like a grain of mustard seed, which, when it is sown in the earth, is less than all the seeds that be in the earth:* [32]*But when it is sown, it groweth up, and becometh greater than all herbs, and shooteth out great branches; so that the fowls of the air may lodge under the shadow of it.*

The mustard seed is one of the tiniest of seeds. It is a precious herb that is used for cooking. Most herbs are small plants and don't become big trees.

But the mustard seed is different: it grows into a big tree wherein many birds take rest. Since it is a precious herb, birds unconsciously know the grandeur of this herbal tree and take rest on it and lodge under the shadow of it. So here also, like a grain of mustard seed, the grain of wisdom-knowledge, which is the knowledge that, thou art the Divine which thou seeketh with all thy heart, takes root within you in your consciousness. When this Truth-awareness is maintained, it leads to the Divine experience. But if you don't maintain this awareness along with the knowledge, then it is dead knowledge; it has no use, except for intellectual purposes wherein you are simply an empty scholar. Thus for this knowledge to take root within you, you have to maintain this awareness. And when you maintain this awareness, it grows and saturates the entire consciousness of yours. In the process the universe too gets permeated with this consciousness.

Thus, in this manner, he was opening out a very great truth. The subtle mystical wisdom-knowledge and its process has been outlined in this section of Chapter 4. Thus you have to give careful thought to it and revisit this section over and over again, and reflect over it, so that you get a clear comprehension as to what it is. Thereby, there is no doubt left in you: You must know the due process of how enlightenment takes place; you don't go through your practical discipline blindly; it is to be gone through with full understanding and knowledge; then only you can confidently proceed on. Therefore, this knowledge is being given and outlined to you by Jesus.

We said that when the harvest time has come, the sickle will be put. We gave the example of Yoga Swami, who was a holy man who had the good fortune to have another holy man put the sickle to make him aware of his Divine nature. Nevertheless, God is your Guru, except in rare instances where God assigns a holy being to effect this due process. Thus never forget that God is your Guru. Of course, you may have a personal guru, but that is a different matter. In the long and final run, it is God who will put the sickle unto you and clear your error.

That is why I started the text with the statement contained in the Gospel of John, "In the beginning was the word; the word was with God; and the word was God". But then I added another sentence that is not found in the Gospel, which was:

When you hear the word from God, it will make you God.

Therefore, you have to go through your own discipline and practices, and when the time comes, you will hear the word from God. How and in what way?

We can answer this question with an analogy… How do you wake up a sleeping man? The answer is, somebody close-by has to call him by name. If the sleeping man's name is Jack, then when you use the word "Jack", only Jack will wake up: if you were to use the name "Peter" or "Robert", then Jack will not wake up, because Jack knows that he is Jack, and therefore when you use the name "Jack", Jack will wake up from his slumber. Similarly also, as far as you are concerned, so far you are in deep slumber to your Divine status. So somebody who is outside this deep slumber must wake you up. And the one who is outside it is God. So at that time, God will wake you up. He has His own process by which He will wake you up. So when you wake up, i.e. when you hear the word from God, you will experience that you are God and know that "I am God". Because, when God speaks to you at that time, He knows in what way He has to speak to you in order to wake you up, as you are in deep slumber to your Divine status.

Therefore, when you hear the word from God, it will make you God. It will awaken you: You will become awakened to your Divine reality from which thus far you were in deep slumber to. That is what is indicated by the phrase "when the harvest has come" – when you are ready. Thus you yourself will have to make yourself ready by putting in the requisite effort, and then only at that time, God will speak to you. That's part of the process.

This section is therefore a very significant section, and you have to revolve it in your mind and understand it as to what its implications are.

Lines 33 and 34:

33And with many such parables spake he the word to them, as they were able to hear it. 34But without a parable spake he not unto them: and when they were alone, he expounded all things to his disciples.

So without a parable, Jesus didn't explain things. Because, one of the best ways of teaching and of bringing out certain truths, is through parables, whereby through a story form, a truth is brought out.

Lines 35-39:

[35]*And the same day, when the even was come, he saith unto them, Let us pass over unto the other side.* [36]*And when they had sent away the multitude, they took him even as he was in the ship. And there were also with him other little ships.* [37]*And there arose a great storm of wind, and the waves beat into the ship, so that it was now full.* [38]*And he was in the hinder part of the ship, asleep on a pillow: and they awake him, and say unto him, Master carest thou not that we perish?* [39]*And he arose and rebuked the wind and said unto the sea, Peace, be still. And the wind ceased, and there was a great calm.*

The sea of Galilee is surrounded by high mountains. As a result, one knows not when a particular storm will come onto the scene. And it can be a swirling storm because of the mountains all around. Even today, it is said that that part of the sea is a little treacherous for people to travel by boat, because of the storms that come that way. So sailors are very careful in navigating that part of the sea.

It is rather strange that Jesus rebuked the wind. You can rebuke another person. You may even rebuke a dog: the dog understands your rebuke. But here Jesus is rebuking the wind – he is scolding the wind. And what's more, he rebukes the sea, as the sea was now in turbulence from the wind. So he first rebuked the wind, then told the sea to be still and be at peace, following which the water became calm.

In the ocean there are two times when the calmness comes. Firstly, before the storm comes there is a calmness, which is a dangerous calmness wherein the calmness precedes an impending storm; it is a mysterious stillness, and the sailors are aware of this. Secondly, after the storm is over, the storm has done its job, and once again calmness settles in.

What happened here? The mega-storm became a mega-peace after Jesus rebuked it and told it to calm down. Jesus spoke to the wind and the sea, and they became calm. And in this action, there is a glorious teaching being brought out.

What Jesus did here was also duplicated on one occasion by the previously mentioned saint of Jaffna, Yoga Swami… He once went into the hills of Sri Lanka in the Kandy area and stayed there for a few weeks. During his stay, there was incessant rain whereby it rained continuously day and night. Yoga Swami got tired of the rain and said to the rains: *"What is this?! You are ceaselessly raining! When will you stop?!"* And lo and behold, the rains immediately stopped. Because, this holy man, for whatever reason, during the course of his life, duplicated many of the miracles which were attributed to Jesus. And this was one particular instance where he did so. So from a mega-storm, a mega-peace comes in.

Now, Jesus used this instance of the storm to give a teaching: "Peace and be still".

Where is your storm raging?

There is a storm raging in the hearts and minds of every individual. And that storm, which is raging, is whipped up by your thoughts, by your passions, by your desires, by your impulses (human and animal impulses), by your ego nature, by your ambitions, and by your intentions to do. All of these are whipping up the storm which is raging in your own mind. And this storm, which is raging in the hearts and minds of people in the form of their desires, passions, thoughts and impulses, must subside. And when it subsides, there will be peace within yourself. And when the peace comes within yourself, then you will be able to be mentally still. So that is why in the Old Testament, it is mentioned, "*Be still, and know that I am God*" (Psalm 46:10).

When you hear it, don't feel shy of your noble, Divine nature inherently present within you. You have come here to manifest your Divine birth-right, which is the treasure hidden from you.

Who told you that you are a sinner?

When Jesus gave sight to the man who was blind from birth, the people around Jesus asked, "*did this man sin or his parents sin for him to be born blind?*" And Jesus replied, "*neither did he nor his parents sin, but he was born thus, to manifest the glory of God.*"

So too, you too, who art so blind to your Divine nature, are thus born so, to manifest "the glory of God".

Therefore, thou art the child of God, or thou are the children of God, eagerly awaiting your Divine inheritance. That is why Jesus declares his mission in Luke 4:18, "*I have come to give sight to the* [spiritually] *blind*" so that they could spiritually see, as "*seeing, they see not*" (Matthew 13:13).

Therefore, Psalm 46:10 is one of the most significant teaching-statements contained in the whole Bible. The entire content of the Bible revolves around it. Both the Old Testament and the New Testament were meant to project this profound truth to the human world. Thus, the Bible has to be re-explored, re-explained and re-taught. And Jesus provides the "key of knowledge" to manifest the kingdom of God in us and around us. Thereby, the purpose of creation is fulfilled. To be Gloried in the Glory of God. Therefore, the entire Bible has to be studied anew, with a fresh and open mind.

"Be still, and know that I am God", therefore, is a very profound statement. This one sentence, with its three features, is the epitome of spiritual wisdom-knowledge and discipline. Be mentally still and be aware that "I am God". If you understand this, no further teaching is required. All that you have to do is maintain the flow of this awareness.

But currently, one cannot be mentally still because of the turbulence in their mind, and this turbulence is present in the hearts and minds of every person. This turbulence will not allow the person to become mentally still. But once you become mentally still, the mega-storm within you, will become a mega-peace.

Thus these three factors follow one another, namely peace, mental stillness and awareness that "I am God". Thus when you are at peace with yourself, you can be mentally still; and when you are mentally still, you can be aware "that I am God". Hence the three go together. Peace leads to mental stillness which in turn enables you to be aware of your God-nature.

With whom should you be at peace with? You have to be at peace with yourself. And you must be at peace with the world around you. And also, you must be at peace with your fellow beings around you. Thus there are three things with which you must be at peace with. It doesn't matter what's going on around you. Do not worry over it. The world is like a dog's tail: you cannot straighten it; you can only straighten and correct yourself. Thus just be at peace with yourself and with the world around you. Also, be at peace with nature. Of course, it is easier to be at peace with nature, which is why people go into nature, as it is peaceful (until a storm comes). Hence be at peace with the surroundings around you. Have no conflict with anybody. Others may have a conflict with you, but you have no conflict with anybody. You psychologically absorb all conflicts thrust upon you, just as Jesus did. Others can produce and bring forth a conflict, but that's their problem: as far as you are concerned, you are at peace with all of them.

Thus being at peace will enable you to be still and to be aware of your Divine nature.

Part 2
The Sower

Lines 1-2:

"¹And he began again to teach by the sea side: and there was gathered unto him a great multitude, so that he entered into a ship, and sat in the sea; and the whole multitude was by the sea on the land. ²And he taught them many things by parables, and said unto them in his doctrine,"

So once again Jesus began to teach by the wayside. And there was a great multitude gathered around listening to him. And since they were compressing him, he had to enter a small boat so he could sit on board the boat and give his teachings to them.

As stated, he taught them *many* parables. Thus many of those parables are not mentioned here.

Because, Jesus' ministry was for three years and a good part of his ministry is not available. But the little that is available is good enough.

This section begins with a very interesting parable: Lines 3-8:

"*3Hearken; Behold, there went out a sower to sow: 4And it came to pass, as he sowed, some fell by the way side, and the fowls of the air came and devoured it up. 5And some fell on stony ground, where it had not much earth; and immediately it sprang up, because it had no depth of earth: 6But when the sun was up, it was scorched; and because it had no root, it withered away. 7And some fell among thorns, and the thorns grew up, and choked it, and it yielded no fruit. 8And other fell on good ground, and did yield fruit that sprang up and increased; and brought forth, some thirty, and some sixty, and some an hundred.*"

This is a very well-known parable. A parable is a particular truth which gets explained in a story form. So via a story form, a hidden truth is brought out and explained by a parable. And that is why Jesus taught in parables: through stories, he explained certain spiritual truths. We will explain the hidden spiritual truth of this parable later.

Line 9:

"And he said unto them, He that hath ears to hear, let him hear."

Of course, those who hear and understand, let them hear.

Lines 10-11:

"10And when he was alone, they that were about him with the twelve asked of him the parable. 11And he said unto them, Unto you it is given to know the mystery of the kingdom of God: but unto them that are without, all these *things are done in parables:"*

The kingdom of God is not to be understood literally as a physical kingdom. The kingdom of heaven means it is heavenly – it is wondrous. The kingdom of God refers to God's kingdom which is the entire universe. And there is a mystery about this kingdom.

The Jews could not understand the meaning of the idea of one being born to be the king, the king of the universe. Instead they took it literally and thought one would be born as the king of the Jews. But the truth is that, it refers to the one who is born to be the king of the universe. And every one of you will be the king of the universe if you understand God's mystery, which is the mystery of the kingdom of God. You have to comprehend the mystical mystery of God's Being. And Jesus is going to use a parable to explain this mystery as to how every one of you can unravel this mystery of the kingdom of God...

But unto those ordinary people around you, who are just casual listeners or passers-by who may listen, parables are given, and let them think and reflect over it, but as far as you are concerned, I will explain them to you, says Jesus.

Line 12:

"That seeing they may see, and not perceive; and hearing they may hear, and not understand; lest at any time they should be converted, and their *sins should be forgiven them."*

When you see this universe, or planet Earth, even though you see it, nevertheless you do not perceive. Not perceive what? That which is the warp and woof of this planet Earth, the truth which is there indeed, the texture. Perceive as what? Perceive as the Divine. It is the Divine Itself which is manifesting Itself to you as the planet Earth and as the universe too. So wherever the planet Earth and the universe are around you, that is said to be where God is to be experienced.

That is why there was a well-known saint in the South of India, known as Seshadri Swamigal, who used to go about in his own peculiar ways. He wouldn't talk much to people. One day when he was in a field looking intently at a buffalo, a villager passed by and asked Seshadri Swamigal, "Swami, are you looking at the buffalo?" And the swami replied, "You buffalo; that is not a buffalo; that is God". That is to say, you are a buffalo because you have a buffalo vision and thereby are seeing a buffalo, but the one who has the God-vision sees it as God.

This is the meaning of the statement "*seeing they may see, and not perceive*". They may see with their eyes but they may not perceive the God-nature present there. "*And hearing they may hear, and not understand*". They may not understand that it is the Divine which is present there.

First, try to understand that it is the Divine which is there so with that Divine vision you can perceive and subsequently experience its hidden Divine content.

And what is this Divine vision? This is very interesting. One is the vision of the multiplicity, which is what you are seeing around you: the plants, the trees, the mountains, the rivers, the clouds, the space, the people, the animals. This is the multiplicity which everyone is seeing. This is world vision. Instead, try to perceive the inherent texture inhering within all manifested phenomena. It is the Divinity in existence that is manifesting to you as the plants, the trees, the mountains, the rivers and the sky too. Therefore, when you perceive, perceive it not with the world vision but with the God-vision.

And what is this God-vision? It is very simple. When you don't have the vision of the multiplicity, then it is God-vision. Be indifferent to the multiplicity. Be indifferent to the names and forms, the things which are differentiating. When you see it, see it not. And then the world vision will begin to recede away.

Because, you've now been told and educated that it is only God there. Try to perceive that. Then the God-vision comes into your foreground. And the world vision recedes into the background. So that is what Jesus is mentioning here.

Seeing they may see but not perceive the Divine. And hearing they may not understand that it is the Divine which is there. When you understand that it is the Divine which is there and it is the Divine which you are perceiving around you, then what will be your reaction or action? Everything that you see will be sacred to you. The entire mother Earth will be sacred. All beings and creatures will be sacred. Everything is sacred. The soil is sacred. The mountains are sacred. The plants and trees are sacred. And accordingly, you would have a corresponding dialogue with all of them.

When you are able to have this corresponding dialogue with all of these things around, your life gets sanctified. Your life gets sanctified by this process. Because, you have got a sanctifying view. Your vision is of a sanctifying nature, which will sanctify everything that you are seeing around. Your new-found God-vision will sanctify everything around you. And in the process, it will sanctify you too.

"[L]*est at any time they should be converted.*" Because, these people are mostly ordinary people because of their worldly passions, worldly desires and their gross nature, and thus will not be able to comprehend it. So these people are not capable of being converted. Converted means to turn around. It is not that you have got to convert a person from one religion to another religion. That is not conversion at all. The real conversion is to convert a man's vision from the world vision to the God-vision. This is the true conversion. For this, you have to turn around or swing around constantly to your

God-vision. Metanoia – turn around and look at your God source. Then, what happens to you? Jesus says, *"and their sins should be forgiven them."*

When you turn around and look at the God source within you, and when your vision is turned around from the world vision to the God-vision and you have the unified vision of Oneness which is pervading and permeating the entire cosmos, then your sins are forgiven.

In the unified field vision of Oneness, you don't see any distinctions. You don't create distinctions amongst humans, such as high and low, big and small. None of these distinctions are there. As far as you are concerned, the entire human race with all its people is of one species. That is the field of Oneness. The social distinctions which you had invented and pursued should all be cleared out of your system in order to have this unified field vision of God. And when you do so, this vision of Oneness or God-vision clears off whatever sins are within you. Atonement is taking place. You're at one with God, which is at-one-ment with God. It is only thereby, that your sins get forgiven. That is how, you die to your SIN. That is why, you who were in-born with SIN, will have to die to your SIN.

You were IN-BORN with SIN because you strayed away (from your God-centre) to the world-vision of multiplicity with an ego-centre. This is SIN and to be living in SIN. The correctional procedure is to be, at-one-ment with God. That is how your sins are atoned.

So how to clear these sins off? It is by atoning for them. How to atone? Be in the state of at-one-ment. When you are at one with your God-nature, you have got the unified field of Oneness, the sameness around. So this field of sameness and Oneness around you has to be cultivated by you in due course by and by.

That is why it is said, God alone is. God alone exists. Wherever there is, it is only God alone who is.

Line 13:

"And he said unto them, Know ye not this parable? and how then will ye know all parables?"

And this is the tragedy indeed. Because, these parables, which have been mentioned in the four gospels of the Bible, have not been properly understood by the human race. Because, it is a mystical teaching. It has to be mystically explained and opened out. And it has to be mystically understood.

This is the primary parable, which opens the way to the comprehension of all other parables. That is why Jesus says, "if you do not understand this parable, how will you understand all other parables?" So therefore, he is explaining this parable of The Sower with the four types of fields. What they are is outlined from line 1-9 and explained thereafter by Jesus in Chapter 4 from the 14th line onwards. But then, in-between, in lines 11 and 12, he unravels the mystery pertaining to the kingdom of God.

Line 14-20:

"14The sower soweth the word. 15And these are they by the way side, where the word is sown; but when they have heard, Satan cometh immediately, and taketh away the word that was sown in their hearts. 16 And these are they likewise which are sown on stony ground; who, when they have heard the word, immediately receive it with gladness; 17And have no root in themselves, and so endure but for a time: afterward, when affliction or persecution ariseth for the word's sake, immediately they are offended. 18And these are they which are sown among thorns; such as hear the word, 19And the cares of this world, and the deceitfulness of riches, and the lusts of other things entering in, choke the word, and it becometh unfruitful. 20And these are they which are sown on good ground; such as hear the word, and receive it, and bring forth fruit, some thirtyfold, some sixty, and some an hundred."

In a field it is the farmer who soweth the seeds, but here the sower soweth the word. The sower here in this instance is the Good Lord. He soweth the word. He injects that word or imparts that word to mankind and to every individual who is so ready to receive it.

What is that word that He soweth in the mind-field of an individual? (The mind is the field in which this particular word is implanted or sown by the Good Lord.) It is a very profound and significant word. The four gospels are going to outline the significance and the implication of that word, and are going to open out what that word is. The entire teaching revolves on that.

And that word is: "You are Gods". Every one of you is the Divine in your real nature, not so in your human nature, but in your true status, everyone is the Divine. In your human nature, you are very much human, *but* in your true status everyone is the Divine. That is why Jesus said in the Gospel of

John, "*...you are Gods*". That is the finale of all teachings which God tells you. Moreover, in the Psalms 82:6, "*you are gods, you are all sons of the Most High.*"

This too is the final essence, the word, the mystic word, which God tells you. In the Upanishads too, the final sentence or the final pronouncement is: "that Divine thou art" *(tat tvam asi)*; that Divine which thou seeketh with all thy heart art thou indeed in your true and essential nature. That is the pronouncement of the Upanishads and so too also that has been reiterated by Jesus in the Gospel of John when he states that "*you are gods*". So if you are Gods, then how to be God?

You did not know that you are God. Therefore, somebody has to come and tell you. All children ask this question: "Mummy, who am I?" It is a natural question. That is one question that is asked. The second question is: Daddy, where am I?" Or "who am I really?" So here too also, that is exactly what the word is all about: it's going to open out this word and state to you that you are the Divine.

In fact, this understanding is the beginning of true religion, wherein you realise and learn to re-alise your oneness or your identity with God. Therefore, this word is being imparted. So it is the Good Lord Himself who sows this word *in your heart*. As, with the mind you understand but it is with your heart that you receive. Thus when you begin to comprehend the significance of your Di-vine nature, you are thereby pleasantly surprised with the Gospel Truth.

And this word, which is the seed-word, is not easily comprehended by everyone. It is only the ones who are psychologically mature who would receive it and understand the significance and the implication of this word that you are the Divine (you are gods), not the others.

Therefore, four types of people were indicated in opening out this parable. In the first instance, when the word is mentioned that you are gods, the first type is those by the wayside who hear when the word is sown. So like the seeds which when sown, fall on the pathways, here too there are people on the wayside, who are just passers-by. They also hear the word when the word is sown. Because, when Jesus spoke, there was a huge multitude made up of the entire range of humanity. And in that range of humanity, you find also people who are just casual listeners. They are those people who are on the wayside who overhear the word.

But when they hear the word, what happens? *"Satan cometh immediately and taketh away the word."* The word "Satan" means your lower impulses which prevent you from accepting the spoken truth. It's too much. When it is said that you are gods, you have got to now act and behave like a God: If you are told that you are a human being and not an animal, you have got to now learn to behave like a human being. But now, if you are told that you are God, then you have got to be godly: it's too much for the simpleton on the streets to receive this news, because he has got to now function and behave like a god which is not possible for him. Therefore, Satan, which refers to his lower impulses, "*taketh away the word*" – immediately the lower impulses lead him away to his usual worldly ways. This word was sown in the mind-field and the heart-field, but the lower impulses come immediately and disregard it. This is one type of people.

"*And these are they likewise which are sown on stony ground.*" The second type of people are likened to the ones wherein the seed is sown on stony ground. On stony ground, there is little earth, not much. "*Who when they have heard the word, immediately receive it with gladness*". So they still have some good tendencies; they have some virtue about them and are nice people. They say, "oh, it's good news to know that I am God; I thought that I was a miserable human being, but here I am told that I am in my essential nature God, so that's good news". So they receive it with gladness, but unfortunately *"they have no root in themselves"*. As, they do not have any foundation within themselves. This word remains with them for a time: When you receive it, for a time it remains in your mind and in your heart, but then what happens is; *"and so endure but for a time: afterward, when affliction or persecution ariseth for the word's sake, immediately they are offended."* So they have received it and are entertaining it for some time, but then, after entertaining and living the implications and concept of this word, afflictions, difficulties and persecutions arise for the sake of this word. But note that you have got to entertain the word, because when you are told you are gods, you have to maintain the awareness of your God-nature. But when afflictions, difficulties and persecutions arise, they immediately give up and say, "it is too much for us;

our worldly problems and difficulties are great indeed". As a result, they quickly give up this word
itself; they just leave it and don't want it. This is
because they have no roots in them; nothing solid
about them. Therefore, they just leave the word
itself: they don't care about it; they receive it but
then dismiss it after some time.

And the third type of person is "*they which are
sown among thorns; such as hear the word*". These are
the people in whom the word is sown in the field
but there are also thorns in the field. "Thorns" here
means the worldly impressions. The word is the
spiritual impression which has been imparted to
you, and the thorns stand for the worldly impressions which are there. What happens is those
worldly impressions which are there smother the
good word which has come because the person is
still very worldly.

"*And the cares of this world, and the deceitfulness of
riches, and the lusts of other things entering in, choke*

the word, and it becometh unfruitful." People are filled with worldly responsibility and cares. They have got a great deal of worldly care in the world. It is no joke to live in the world. To take care of oneself is a big problem. To take care of two people is a bigger problem. And if you have a family, what a big problem it is! As, you are constantly occupied with taking care of the family, day and night. Day or night you have got to now take care of this family of yours. You've got to care for your working field, you've got to care for your house and many other things.

And not only that. There is the deceitfulness of richness, which is the glamour of the world. The glamour of the world is still enticing people. That is why God has created a glamorous world. You may call it *maya*. *Maya* means that which fascinates and entertains you and captures your interest. So the world has so captured your interest in so many ways, and as a result of this, you don't care to entertain this word. So one is the cares of this world and the second is the deceitfulness of riches.

And then there is the "lusts of other things" whereby the person is filled with desires and passions: you've got so many desires and passions, and all of this fills you up. All these three factors choke this word and do not allow this word to take fertile root or ground in the heart and mind of the individual, just like the bushes and thorns choking the seed which is trying to emerge out as a little plant. The majority of the human race is caught in this section. They are good people and nice people, but they are preoccupied with the world or with the glamour of the world, and some are involved with the passions of the world and want to fulfil their desires; and their passions overtake them. As a result, the word gets choked up and it becomes unfruitful. The word doesn't take root in their minds and hearts.

Then, thereafter, you have the fourth type of individual wherein the word takes good root in them. *"And these are they that are sown on good ground."* So the good people, wherein they are good, noble and righteous, have the seed, or word of God, sown on good ground or good soil. Good soil means a soil which has been prepared.

You know very well that a farmer, when he goes to sow the seed in the field, has to prepare the bed of the soil so that he can plant the seeds therein: he prepares the bed of the soil; he waters it; he tills the soil and oxidises it. Though today they plough it with tractors, in the olden days it was done with ploughs. Thus they prepare the bed of the soil so that the soil can receive the good seed when it falls on it.

So here also, these people, who are noble, righteous, God-loving, God-fearing, of a good nature, incapable of doing wrong things, are those who have prepared their soil. These are the people of virtue and goodness who have prepared their hearts and their minds by righteous living. And that is why righteous living is very important in a man's life. Juxtaposed to this, is unrighteous living wherein a wrong source of income has been obtained. This ill-gotten income corrupts the mind, and this is so stated in the Old Testament as a follow-up to the commandments and injunctions of righteous life.

Therefore, corrupt income corrupts and perverts the mind, and therefore the income has to be a good, noble and righteous income. That is why Lord Buddha emphasised Right Livelihood in his Eightfold Path. Right Livelihood is that wherein you do not cause harm, misery or difficulties to others in making your livelihood in life. This is a very important feature.

A good and honourable person will see to it that his living and livelihood is on the right direction. These are the people who have prepared the bed of their soil for the good seed to be sown in. The field of operations in which the word is sown is the mind-field and the heart field; thus these are people with a good, clean and pure heart. Three things have to be clean here: you have to have a clean mind, a clean heart and a clean hand.

When you do things with your hand, it should be a clean hand which does things in a correct and righteous manner. So by this process of having a clean mind, a clean heart and a clean hand, the soil of your mind and heart get prepared for the reception and the dawn of the good word. And the good word is that "you are the Divine". These are the people referred to as the good soil wherein the word is sown on good ground. They hear the word and receive it, and having received it, *"bring forth fruit, some thirtyfold, some sixty, and some an hundred."* That's very interesting.

When they receive the word, they entertain the word in their heart and in their mind. How? By becoming God-aware. That's the way to entertain it. Formerly they were aware of this and that: they were aware of the world, they were aware of other things, but now instead of all the other things, they have now become aware of their Divine nature, the *Atman* or *Brahman*. (*Brahman* is the term used for the Divine; it is not a name for God but is a term by which the Divine is to be understood because the word has got enormous metaphysical meaning behind it.)

Once the teacher, the Messiah, makes the pronouncement "you are gods", then it is left to the disciples to feel that "I am the Divine; I am God (*Aham Brahmasmi)*" wherein you maintain that awareness of your God-nature. For you to so maintain the awareness of your God-nature, you have to forget your individual human self – you are no more this individual human self, this miserable little fellow, but you are the glorious Divine, so leave that guy alone and feel your God-nature. By that you forget the world – you're not interested anymore in the world or the proceedings of the world; let the world go its own way; it doesn't matter what it is. When you can constantly maintain this awareness, this is called in simple English as God-awareness. And if you were to reduce it into technical metaphysical terms, it is the awareness where there is nothing there: the content of that awareness has got nothing there – there is nothingness in that awareness; only simple, pure awareness is present; you are not aware of the world, you are not aware of yourself and the problems of yourself. Also, you are not concerned with the world and its problems; you have forgotten that. And you have also forgotten the third thing, which when I mention, people are a little diffident about it; that is, you forget all the religious indoctrination that you have had so far; just forget it once and for all; you are God; you are not a Christian nor a Hindu nor a Buddhist nor anybody else; you are the Divine; so lose and give up that religious identity also. Just be yourself in your Divine nature. Just be your true Divine self. To be so, just be so. Be "I AM". And just maintain the flow of this Am-ness. This flow of Am-ness will lead you to your blessed state.

The significance of this "I AM" state was illustrated by God to Moses, in the "Burning Bush" episode in the Book of Exodus. Therein when Moses asked the unseen speaking God, His identity, God replied, "Tell them, 'I AM WHO I AM'". This is the greatest mantra given to the human race by God. God in declaring Himself wants every man, to so affirm his or her own Divine Am-ness, inherently present within. Just as God declared Himself, so also God wants every God-loving man to similarly do so and be so. That is, to be in one's own Am-ness. This statement was an education imparted by God to man.

Maintaining this Am-ness in technical language is called *Brahmakaravritti*: That is the mind assuming the form of the formless *Brahman*. That's one way of putting it. Another way of stating it in Christian terminology is, you are maintaining the Holy Sabbath. Because, man was made in the image of God. So since God has no images, when you are in an imageless state, you are automatically in the imageless image of God. Then at that time, your mind has synchronised itself with the nature of God. That is, you are in communion with God. Or we could also say, this is the time when you are in holy communion.

So whenever you meditate, your mind has become very silent, silent to all mental and worldly phenomena, and is only maintaining this pure, unqualified awareness. When it does so, you are in holy communion with God. So when this happens, and when you keep maintaining this state day in day out for the rest of your life, you bring forth fruit, the fruit of your labour. This is your labour. The hard labour that you are going through in maintaining this awareness.

And then you *"bring forth fruit, some thirtyfold, some sixty, and some an hundred."* So that one little seed, which is the impression that "I am the Divine", keeps on increasing. That is to say, every time you maintain this awareness, you are entertaining and cultivating Divine impressions within yourself. Like drops of water filling up an empty bucket, your mind is being saturated with God-impressions. Gradually this goes and fills up your mind, and in doing so, this Divine-impression clears out all the worldly impressions. This is what is happening there: your worldly impressions are being cleared and your mind is being saturated with the Divine impression. That is why he says, *"bring forth fruit, some thirtyfold, some sixty, and some an hundred."* The process keeps increasing until you reach a saturation level wherein the Divine impression has saturated your frame of mind.

This is the meaning of the Parable of the Seed which has been sown into you by the Good Lord. It is only when you are a good and righteous person, this increase happens – this is the fourth category of persons on whom the good seed is sown. This process is the foundation of true religion.

Moreover, in your life, there is not only a spiritual foundation, but there is also a worldly foundation. You require both. The worldly foundation is contained in the Ten Commandments. Actually, there are more than ten: there are about twenty-four commandments. And the spiritual foundation is wherein you cultivate spiritual virtues which are beautifully and explicitly stated by Jesus in the Sermon on the Mount. Therefore, both are necessary.

And in doing so, you are preparing the soil for the seed to germinate and grow. So this is the foundation of life. And the Old Testament is all about worldly commandments. While, the New Testament is talking about the spiritual foundation. So one is the basis of the other. Both are necessary.

Then he says with another parable in line 21:
"And he said unto them, Is a candle brought to be put under a bushel, or under a bed? and not to be set on a candlestick?"

A candle is not to be hidden but is to be set on a candlestick. And what is the candlestick? You are the candlestick. You will find that when you go to the church, there is candlestand wherein you light the candle in the church. Similarly, if you go to the temple, there is a temple lamp which you light to giveth light. So here also, you are the candlestick. And this candlestick is lighted with God-awareness.

So you are the candlestick, and in your mind itself, in your awareness, this lamp of wisdom-knowledge has been lit. As a result of this, it will illuminate you and illuminate the entire universe in due course. This will get explained by Jesus subsequently. He is now unfolding the parables one after the other. Each one is succeeding the other. In this section of Chapter 4, one parable leads to another.

In this parable of the candlestick, you are the candlestick in which the God-awareness is maintained, and this goes to light up yourself. Because, you are in darkness, as you do not know who you are. Also, at the same time, the world around you, which was in darkness, is now lit up with God-awareness. That is the light. Therefore, this parable of just a few lines is also given in this section.

Line 22:

"For there is nothing hid, which shall not be manifested; neither was any thing kept secret, but that it should come abroad."

What is that which is hidden? God's beingness. God's natural state of existence has been hidden to you by the objective world which is around you – this world of multiplicity of various names and forms has hidden the existence of God which is intrinsically there. Therefore, when you maintain this God-awareness or God-vision, which is the unified vision of Oneness, which is whole and non-fragmented, then the multiplicity of the universe disappears: When you perceive the entire world with this unfragmented, wholistic vision of Oneness, then the fragmented vision of the multiplicity, which was until now in the foreground, begins to recede into the background. Thus you've now brought in a new vision: The God-vision. The unified vision of Oneness. This is called non-dual awareness: the duality of I and you, and the duality of I and the universe, is no more there. When you begin to maintain this, the awareness of multiplicity begins to recede into the background and the non-dual awareness comes into the foreground.

This is the meaning of the said phrase "*there is nothing hid, which shall not be manifested*". Therefore, when you maintain and entertain this over a period of time, as years roll by, then what happens is, the unmanifest Divine, which was previously hidden by the names and forms of the world, begins to manifest to you. Where you were previously seeing the world, you will be seeing the Divine everywhere around you.

And also, at the same time, they said it was secret knowledge. The knowledge that "I am that Divine" was secret knowledge. Your individual nature, or your identification with your individual nature, was covering your Divine nature. But when you begin to maintain the "I am the Divine" awareness with your eyes closed, then what happens is, the "I am the Divine" awareness saturates your mind and consciousness whereby the sense of your individuality recedes into the background and disappears. Thereafter, the "I am the Divine" experience manifests as a matter of inner experience. This is what is implied in the phrase "*neither was any thing kept secret, but that it should come abroad.*"

Thus, "*it should come abroad*" means that It should manifest Itself. Therefore, both within yourself and outside yourself, you'll experience the Divine. Thus the objective world will manifest as the Divine, so too the subjective individual as well. This is what Jesus is indicating here, but it is worded in a mystical manner, not directly.

Therefore, he says in line 23:
"*If any man have ears to hear, let him hear.*"

If you've got the good ears to understand this, then you better hear it: This is profound knowledge indeed, and if you've got the benediction or the good fortune to comprehend and understand this, you better hear this and live by it.

Then in line 24 he says:

"And he said unto them, Take heed what ye hear: with what measure ye mete, it shall be measured to you: and unto you that hear shall more be given."

Be careful of what you hear because what you hear is something very important and very significant. If you hear something remarkably good, take heed of it because it will transform and transmute your life. So take heed what you hear.

The phrase *"with what measure ye mete, it shall be measured to you"* has both a worldly meaning and a mystical meaning. The worldly meaning is: as per what you do, you will receive; with the measure you judge things and go about your operations in life, accordingly it will be given unto you. Then there is the mystical meaning too...

When you have a ground, you measure it. The Earth-field is the ground. The entire universe and the Earth are the field or the ground of your operations. What is the measure with which you are going to measure this universe? With God's measure. So you envelop this mighty world, which is huge and vast, with God-awareness. With God-awareness, you measure it. You fill it up. The entire infinite expanding universe is going to be measured by you with one simple measure called the God-measure.

And *"it shall be measured to you"*. So if you measure it with the God-measure, then it shall be returned to you: in return you will experience God there. Because, you are measuring the world with this God-vision, so in that same manner, it shall be measured to you with the God-experience. So when you view the whole universe with this God-vision, in due course, you will have the God-experience. And *"unto you that hear shall more be given"*. And those that hear this, and comprehend and understand this, will have more truths imparted unto them. Because, you are in the position to comprehend it and to comprehend further truths.

However, in line 25, Jesus is bringing a word of caution:

"For he that hath, to him shall be given: and he that hath not, from him shall be taken even that which he hath."

For, he that has this God-awareness, will be given more: he will be given that capacity to maintain this God-awareness more and more. As you keep on maintaining this, you will develop the capacity and the ability to maintain this awareness more and more. But if you have this awareness and do not sustain it due to your preoccupation with the world and other interests and pastimes, and thereby do not maintain or cultivate this awareness, then even that which you have, will be taken away from you. Hence, as the Good Lord says, that person who does not go about maintaining this awareness day in and day out in a consistent manner, even that which he has will be taken away from him.

This all of you know very well... Especially in the field of sports, when you attain a certain capacity, you've got to keep it going: if you do not practice your sport, then you begin to lose your ability to get back to your original true form – you are losing that capacity. Therefore, to sustain it, you have got to consistently keep on practicing it until the end result is obtained. The end result is enlightenment. Until that is obtained, one should keep on sustaining this. But if a person does not go through this consistently, then even what he has will fade away from him. And herein, the second law of thermodynamics in physics, which is the law of entropy, comes into the picture...

Any organised entity, if is not maintained and sustained, undergoes gradual deterioration in due time and in due course. That is, decay takes place. It is an automatic process. It is a natural in-built process, an in-built law. An automatic deterioration takes place.

And that is why the Muslim, no matter where he is, even if in an airport, sees to it that he goes through his *namas* three times a day. He doesn't care who is around: even in the airport he spreads his mat, kneels down in prayer and does his *namas*. What a wonderful thing. He is sustaining and maintaining this.

So that is what the Good Lord is saying here… If you do not sustain and maintain this, then it will deteriorate within yourself – even that ability which you had will go away.

Then he says in line 26:
"And he said, So is the kingdom of God, as if a man should cast seed into the ground;"

So the kingdom of God is likened to a growing mustard seed, stated as an example as how you too can arrive at the kingdom of God within you and around you. And Jesus has outlined this with the beautiful simile of the mustard seed.

Made in the USA
Las Vegas, NV
12 December 2021

37299370R00049